Garden Medley Quilts

*Make a Sampler and
24 Coordinating Projects*

Johanna Wilson

All American **Crafts** Publishing, Inc
"The Creative Experience"

Garden Medley Quilts

Make a Sampler and 24 Coordinating Projects

Text © 2007 by Johanna Wilson
Artwork © 2007 All American Crafts, Inc.

All American Crafts Publishing, Inc.
7 Waterloo Road
Stanhope, NJ 07874
www.allamericancrafts.com

Publisher • **Jerry Cohen**

Chief Executive Officer • **Darren Cohen**

Art Director • **Kelly Albertson**

Editor • **Nicole Gould**

Photography • **Double D Photoworks** and
Van Zandbergen Photography

Technical Illustrator • **Kathleen Govaerts**

Product Development Director • **Vivian Rothe**

Vice President/Quilt Advertising & Marketing • **Carol Newman**

Printed in USA

ISBN-13: 978-0-9789513-2-0
ISBN-10: 0-9789513-2-8
Library of Congress Control Number: 2007937475

Welcome

Dear Friends,

My niece, Jen, called me recently to say that she was on her way to the quilt store to buy backing for a baby quilt for a friend's baby shower the next day – how much would she need?

It seems only a short time ago that she was a youngster sitting at my sewing machine making quilt blocks from my stash. How blessed I am that she enjoys quilting too and has encouraged her friends to join in our common hobby. Quilting is a creative process that provides all of us with a way to express ourselves while making beautiful and useful projects, gifts, and masterpieces.

Quilters are very special. They love to shop for fabric, attend classes and quilt shows, and make quilts for family, friends, and worthy organizations. But most of all, quilters love to share, everything from new quilt shops, fabric sales, and indispensable tools to tried and true techniques, joys, and sorrows.

Teaching quilting has many rewards, the most notable being the knowing look when color choices, piecing, and finishing create a lovely project. The "I did it!" moment and the "What if I …" opportunities.

The *Garden Medley Sampler Quilt* was designed for one of my summer quilt retreats in Minnesota. It offers the quilter an opportunity to learn and use many techniques to create a quilt of many different blocks. The collection of quilts in this book includes the original sampler and additional quilts made from one or more of the Garden Medley Sampler blocks. There are quilts in many sizes, shapes, and colors. There are quilts for beds, walls, tabletops, and pillows. There are quilts for all levels of expertise.

I hope you will make one, two, or more of these projects and enjoy the thrill of quiltmaking as much as I do. Most of all, I hope you will continue to share this joy with others.

Johanna Wilson

c o n t

ents

Garden Medley Sampler Quilt

This stunning sampler quilt was originally created for a three-day retreat. The differing blocks provide an opportunity to challenge yourself as a quilter, trying out new techniques and methods ... and you won't get bored with the variety of blocks used!

Finished size 92½" x 92½"

Materials

- 2 yards A floral border
- 3 yards B green inner border and binding
- 2 yards C tan sashing
- 1¾ yards D background #1 lightest
- ½ yard E background #2 lighter
- ¾ yard F background #3 light
- ½ yard G brown print
- ¾ yard H red print
- ¾ yard I medium blue
- ½ yard J navy
- 1 yard K medium green

Cutting Borders

If you are planning on piecing the sampler as shown, it is a good idea to cut your borders first. That way, you can cut them in lengthwise sections and avoid piecing them.

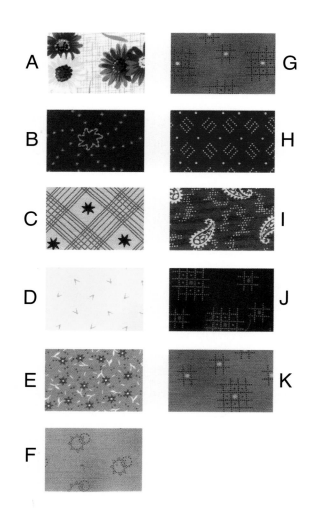

A fabric chart helps keep large projects organized.

Four-Patch on Point #1

Make two blocks, 8½" x 8½" unfinished

Cutting

From the navy print J:
1: 1¾" x 16" strip
4: 3" squares

From the red print H:
1: 1¾" x 16" strip

From the medium blue print I:
4: 6½" squares, cut once on the diagonal

Directions

1. Sew 1¾" x 16" J and H strips, right sides together, along the long edge. Press toward J.

2. Cut at 1¾" intervals. Make 8 cuts (1¾" x 3").

3. Sew two cuts together to make a four-patch (3" x 3"). Make 4.

4. Sew a 3" J square to each four-patch (3" x 5½"). Press toward the square. Make 4.

5. Sew pairs together to make a four-patch (5½" x 5½"). Make 2.

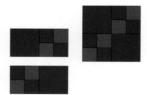

6. Center one I triangle on opposite sides of each four-patch. Press toward the triangles. (See page 121 for tips on centering.)

7. Repeat with the remaining sides of each triangle. Press toward the triangles.

8. Trim each square to measure 8½" x 8½". **Note:** There is no sashing on this block.

Four-Patch on Point #2

Make two blocks, 8½" x 8½" unfinished

Cutting

From the navy print J:
  1: 1¾" x 16" strip

From the medium blue print I:
  1: 1¾" x 16" strip
  4: 3" squares

From the red print H:
  4: 6½" squares, cut once on the diagonal

From the tan sashing print:
  2: 3½" x 8½" rectangles

Directions

1. Sew 1¾" x 16" J and I strips, right sides together, along the long edge. Press toward J.

2. Cut at 1¾" intervals. Make 8 cuts (1¾" x 3").

3. Sew two cuts together to make a four-patch (3" x 3"). Make 4.

4. Sew a 3" I square to each four-patch (3" x 5½"). Press toward the square. Make 4.

5. Sew pairs together to make a four-patch (5½" x 5½"). Make 2.

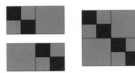

6. Center one H triangle on opposite sides of each four-patch. Press toward the triangles. (See page 121 for tips on centering.)

7. Repeat with the remaining sides of each triangle. Press toward the triangles.

8. Trim each square to measure 8½" x 8½".

9. Sew one 3½" x 8½" C sashing to the each block. Make 2 (8½" x 11½").

Basket #1 Pieced Handle

Make two blocks, 8½" x 8½" unfinished

Cutting

From the floral border fabric A:
  1: 5" square, cut once on the diagonal

From the green border fabric B:
  1: 5" square, cut once on the diagonal
  7: 3" squares, cut once on the diagonal

From the lightest background fabric D:
  7: 3" squares, cut once on the diagonal
  4: 2½" x 4½" rectangles
  2: 2½" squares

From the tan sashing fabric C:
  4: 2½" x 8½" rectangles

Directions

1. Sew 5" B and A triangles together along the bias edge. Press toward B. Make 2. Trim to 4½" x 4½".

2. Sew B and D triangles together along the bias edge. Press toward B. Make 14. Trim to 2½" x 2½".

3. Sew pairs of B/D triangle squares together. Make 2. Note orientation.

4. Sew one pair to each center A/B triangle. Press toward the center.

5. Sew 3 B/D triangle squares together. Make 2. Note orientation.

6. Sew the B/D triangle squares to the adjacent side of the center. Press toward the small triangles.

7. Sew a triangle square to one end of 4½" D rectangle. Press toward the rectangle. Make 2 (2½" x 6½").

8. Sew one rectangle to the bottom of the basket. Make 2.

9. Sew a triangle square to one end of the remaining 4½" D rectangle. Note orientation. Press toward the triangle. Make 2 (2½" x 6½").

10. Sew a D square to the D side of a B/D triangle square. Press toward the triangle square.

11. Sew the rectangle to the basket. Press. Make 2 (8½" x 8½").

12. Sew a 2½" x 8½" C sashing strip to the top and bottom of each basket. Note orientation. Make 2 (8½" x 12½").

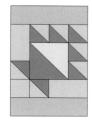 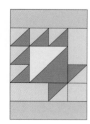

Basket #2 Appliquéd Handle

Make two blocks, 8½" x 8½" unfinished

Cutting

From the lightest background fabric D:
- **1:** 5¼" square, cut twice on the diagonal
- **2:** 4½" x 8½" rectangles

From the light background F:
- **1:** 5¼" square, cut twice on the diagonal
- **1:** 6½" square, cut once on the diagonal
- **2:** 1½" x 15" bias strips (must be on the bias!)

Directions

1. Sew 5¼" D and F triangles together along the short side. Note orientation. Make 2.

2. Sew the D/F triangle to the left side of the large F triangle. Make 2.

3. Sew F and D triangles together along the short side. Note orientation. Make 2.

4. Sew the F/D triangle to the right side of the large F triangle. Make 2.

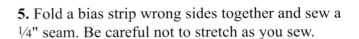

5. Fold a bias strip wrong sides together and sew a ¼" seam. Be careful not to stretch as you sew.

6. Slip a cardboard strip (or bias bar) inside the bias strip handle, turning the seam to one side of the cardboard. Press with the cardboard inside the handle. Remove the cardboard and repress, without stretching. Mark the center of the handle. Make 2.

7. Fold a D rectangle in half. Find and mark the center. Position the handle appropriately.

8. Pin the handle in place, beginning and ending at least ½" from edges to allow for the seam allowance.

9. Stitch by hand or by machine. Make 2 handle pieces.

10. Sew the two halves of the block together. Press. Make 2 (8½" x 8½").

11. Sew an elongated four-patch (see page 19) to the top of one basket. Reverse for the second basket. Make 1 each (8½" x 11½").

 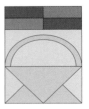

Log Cabin #1

Make two blocks, 12½" x 8½" unfinished

Cutting

From the red print H:
   2: 2½" x 3½" rectangles

From the lightest background D:
   4: 1½" x 3½" rectangles

From the medium green K:
   4: 2" x 4½" rectangles

From the lighter background E;
   4: 1½" x 6½" rectangles

From the navy print J:
   4: 2 x 6½" rectangles

From the floral border fabric A:
   4: 1½" x 9½" rectangles

From the medium blue print I:
   4: 2" x 8½" rectangles

Directions

Note: Press all seams away from the center.

1. Sew a 1½" x 3½" D rectangle to the top and bottom of a 3½" x 2½" H center. Make 2 (3½" x 4½"). Press.

2. Sew a 2" x 4½" K rectangle to each side of the center. Make 2 (4½" x 6½"). Press.

3. Sew a 1½" x 6½" E rectangle to the top and bottom of the center. Make 2 (6½" x 6½"). Press.

4. Sew a 2" x 6½" J rectangle to each side of the center. Make 2 (6½" x 9½"). Press.

5. Sew a 1½" x 9½" A rectangle to the top and bottom of the center. Make 2 (8½" x 9½"). Press.

6. Sew a 2" x 8½" I rectangle to each side of the center. Make 2 (8½" x 12½"). Press.

Tips for Making Log Cabin Blocks

1. Press from the center out after each color is added.

2. Check to be sure you are not adding pleats as you press. Working from the top and holding the last sewn piece at an angle from the iron may help.

3. Check for the correct size after each round to see if your measurements match the ones given.

Remember: *An eighth of an inch multiplied by the number of seams in the block can change the size of the block significantly!*

Log Cabin #2

Make two blocks, 8½" x 12½" unfinished

Cutting

From the red print H:
   2: 2½" x 3½" rectangles

From the medium green print K:
   4: 1½" x 3½" rectangles

From the lightest background D:
   4: 2" x 4½" rectangles

From the navy print J:
   4: 1½" x 6½" rectangles

From the lighter background E:
   4: 2" x 6½" rectangles

From the medium blue print I:
   4: 1½" x 9½" rectangles

From the floral border print A:
   4: 2" x 8½" rectangles

Directions

Note: Press all seams away from the center. See Tips for Making Log Cabin Blocks, previous page.

1. Sew a 1½" x 3½" K rectangle to each side of a 2½" x 3½" H center. Make 2 (3½" x 4½"). Press.

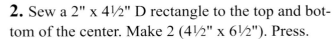

2. Sew a 2" x 4½" D rectangle to the top and bottom of the center. Make 2 (4½" x 6½"). Press.

3. Sew a 1½" x 6½" J rectangle to each side of the center. Make 2 (6½" x 6½"). Press.

4. Sew a 2" x 6½" E rectangle to the top and bottom of the center. Make 2 (6½" x 9½"). Press.

5. Sew a 1½" x 9½" I rectangle to each side of the center. Make 2 (8½" x 9½"). Press.

6. Sew a 2" x 8½" A rectangle to the top and bottom of the center. Make 2 (8½" x 12½"). Press.

Clover #1

Make two blocks, 12½" x 12½" unfinished

Cutting

From the lightest background D:
  11: 3" squares, cut once on the diagonal
  4: 7" squares, cut once on the diagonal

From the medium blue print I:
  9: 3" squares, cut once on the diagonal
  2: 2½" x 10" rectangles
  2: 2½" squares

From the red print H:
  2: 4½" squares
  2: 5" squares, cut once on the diagonal

From the tan sashing fabric C:
  2: 2½" x 12½" rectangles

Directions

1. Sew 3" D and I triangles together along the bias edge. Press. Trim to 2½" x 2½". Make 18 D/I triangle squares.

2. Sew a pair of D/I triangles squares together. Note orientation. Make 2.

3. Sew a pair of D/I triangle squares to a 4½" H square. Make 2.

4. Sew three D/I triangle squares together. Note orientation. Make 2.

5. Sew to the adjacent side of the center. Make 2 (6½" x 6½").

6. Sew a pair of D/I triangle squares together. Note orientation. Make 2.

7. Sew a 3" D triangle to the end of the D/I triangle squares. Make 2.

8. Sew this strip to 5" H triangle. Make 2.

9. Center and sew a 7" D triangle to the triangle piece. Press. Make 2. Trim to 6½" x 6½".

10. Repeat steps 6-9, changing the direction of the triangles, as shown. Make 2. Trim to 6½" x 6½".

11. Center and sew a 2½" x 10" I strip between two 7" D triangles. Make 2. Trim square to 6½" x 6½".

12. Arrange the squares and sew together in pairs. Sew the pairs together to create the clover block. Make 2 (12½" x 12½").

13. Sew a 2½" I square on the diagonal at the bottom of the stem.

14. Sew a 2½" x 12½" C sashing at the bottom of each block. Note orientation.

Clover #2

Make two blocks, 12½" x 12½" unfinished

Cutting

From the lightest background D:
  11: 3" squares, cut once on the diagonal
  4: 7" squares, cut once on the diagonal

From the red print H:
  9: 3" squares, cut once on the diagonal
  2: 2½" x 10" rectangles
  2: 2½" squares

From the medium blue print I:
  2: 4½" squares
  2: 5" squares, cut once on the diagonal

From the tan sashing fabric C:
  2: 2½" x 12½" rectangles

Directions

1. Sew 3" D and H triangles together along the bias edge. Press. Trim to 2½" x 2½". Make 18 D/H triangle squares.

2. Sew a pair of D/H triangles squares together. Note orientation. Make 2.

3. Sew a pair of D/H triangle squares to a 4½" I square. Make 2.

4. Sew three D/H triangles squares together. Note orientation. Make 2.

5. Sew the D/H triangle squares to the adjacent side of the center. Make 2 (6½" x 6½").

6. Sew a pair of D/H triangle squares together. Note orientation. Make 2.

7. Sew a 3" D triangle to the end of the D/H triangle squares. Make 2.

8. Sew this strip to a 5" I triangle. Make 2.

9. Center and sew a 7" D triangle to the triangle piece. Press. Make 2. Trim to 6½" x 6½".

10. Repeat steps 6-9, changing the direction of the triangles, as shown. Make 2. Trim to 6½" x 6½".

11. Center and sew a 2½" x 10" H strip between two 7" D triangles. Make 2. Trim square to 6½" x 6½".

12. Arrange the squares and sew together in pairs. Sew the pairs together to create the clover block. Make 2 (12½" x 12½").

13. Sew a 2½" H square on the diagonal at the bottom of the stem.

14. Sew a 2½" x 12½" C sashing at the bottom of each block. Note orientation.

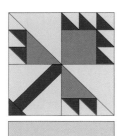

Star Lily

Make two blocks, 8½" x 7½" unfinished

Cutting

From the medium green print K:
    4: 2¼" x 4" rectangles
    16: 2¼" squares

From the floral border print A:
    2: 1½" x 4" rectangles

From the lightest background D:
    4: 2¼" x 4" rectangles
    4: 2¼" x 5" rectangles
    8: 2¼" squares

Directions

1. Sew a 2¼" x 4" K rectangle to each side of a 1½" x 4" A center. Make 2 (5" x 4"). Press toward the center.

2. Sew a 2¼" K square on the diagonal to one end of a 2¼" x 4" D rectangle. Note the angle. Make 4.

3. Sew a 2¼" K square on the diagonal on the other end of the same rectangle. Note the angle.

4. Sew one rectangle to each side of the center block. Make 2 (8½" x 5").

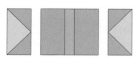

5. Sew a 2¼" K square on the diagonal to the end of 2¼" x 5" D rectangle. Make 4.

6. Sew a 2¼" K square on the diagonal to the other end of the same rectangle.

7. Sew a 2¼" D square to each end of the rectangles.

8. Sew one strip to the top and bottom of the center. Make 2 (8½" x 7½").

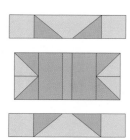

Twister

Make two blocks, 12½" x 12½" unfinished

Cutting

From the lightest background fabric D:
    8: 3½" squares, cut once on the diagonal
    8: 2¾" x 8" rectangles
    4: 3¼" squares, cut once on the diagonal

From the red print H:
    8: 3½" squares, cut once on the diagonal

From the navy print J:
    2: 3" squares

From the medium green print K:
    4: 3¼" squares, cut once on the diagonal

Directions

1. Sew the 3½" D and H triangles together. Press flat, open seams, and press again carefully. Make 16. Trim to 3"x 3".

2. Sew a D/H triangle square to each side of a 3" J square. Note orientation. Press toward the square. Make 2 (3" x 8").

3. Sew 3 D/H triangle squares together in a row. Note orientation. Make 4 (3" x 8").

4. Sew one row to the top and one to the bottom of the center row. Make 2 (8 x 8").

5. Sew a 2¾" x 8" D rectangle to the sides of the blocks. Press to the rectangles (8" x 12½").

6. Sew the 3¼" D and K triangles together. Press flat, open seams, and press again carefully. Trim to 2¾". Make 8.

7. Sew one D/K triangle square to each end of a 2¾" x 8" D rectangle. Note orientation. Make 4 (2¾" x 12½").

8. Sew one to the top and bottom of the center piece to complete the Twister blocks. Make 2 (12½" x 12½").

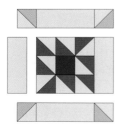

Puzzle

Make two blocks, 12½" x 8½" unfinished

Cutting

From the medium green print K:
  4: 2½" squares
  4: 2½" x 4½" rectangles

From the medium blue print I:
  4: 2½" squares
  4: 2½" x 4½" rectangles

From the lightest background D:
  4: 2½" squares
  4: 2½" x 4½" rectangles

From the red print H:
  4: 2½" squares
  4: 2½" x 4½" rectangles

Directions

1. Sew 2½" K and I squares together. Make 4 (2½" x 4½").

2. Sew an I rectangle and a K rectangle to the sides of the squares. Press toward the center. Make 4 (6½" x 4½").

3. Sew 2½" D and H squares together. Make 4 (2½" x 4½").

4. Sew an H rectangle and a D rectangle to the sides of the squares. Press toward the rectangles. Make 4 (6½" x 4½").

5. Arrange and sew the blocks in pairs with K and D facing each other. Make 4 pairs (6½" x 8½").

6. Arrange and sew the pairs together. Make 2 (12½" x 8½").

Checkerboard Spacers

Make four blocks, 4½" x 8½" unfinished and twelve blocks, 4½" x 12½" unfinished

Cutting

From the lighter background E:
   3: 2½" x WOF

From the brown print G:
   3: 2½" x WOF

Directions

1. Sew the 2½" E and G strips together along the long side. Make three sets. Press toward E.

2. Cut at 2½" intervals. Make 24 (2½" x 4½"). Save the remaining strip set for later.

3. Sew 6 cuts together, alternating fabric to make the Checkerboard Spacers (4½" x 12½"). Make 4.

4. Sew a 4½" x 12½" Checkerboard Spacer above and below each Twister block. Make 2. (12½" x 20½").

5. Cut the remaining E/G strip at 4½" intervals. Make 8 (4½" x 4½").

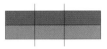

6. Sew 2 cuts together, alternating fabric to make 4 elongated four-patches (4½" x 8½").

Make 2 of each orientation. Set aside for use with Basket #2 and Sunflower blocks.

Combine Checkerboard Spacer blocks to create the Hopscotch Baby Quilt *on page 92.*

Sunflower Block

Make three blocks, 8½" x 18½" unfinished

Cutting

From the lighter background E:
 12: 1½" squares
 3: 3¼" squares

From the brown print G:
 3: 4½" squares

From the light background F:
 6: 3¼" squares
 24: 1½" squares

From the lightest background D:
 3: 3¼" squares
 24: 1½" x 2½" rectangles
 12: 2½" squares
 3: 8½" x 10½" rectangles

From the green border fabric B:
 3: 1½" x 13" bias strips (must be on the bias!)

From the medium green print K:
 Scraps for leaves

From the tan sashing fabric C:
 2: 3½" x 8½" rectangles

Directions

1. Sew a 1½" E square on the diagonal on opposite corners of each 4½" G square. Repeat with the remaining two corners. Make 3.

2. Draw a diagonal line on each 3¼" F square.

3. Place F square right sides together with 3¼" D square. Make 3.

4. Sew a seam ¼" on each side of the drawn line. Press.

5. Cut on the drawn line. Open and press toward F. Make 6 triangle squares.

6. Repeat with the 3¼" F and E squares. Make 6 triangles squares.

7. Draw a line, corner to corner, perpendicular to the seam on the D/F triangle squares only.

8. Place one of each E/F combination right sides together with the D/F triangles on the top.

9. Butt F seams together, opposite one another. Stitch ¼" on each side of the drawn line. Press.

10. Cut on the line to make 12 X blocks. Press again. Trim each to 2½". Set aside.

11. Sew a 1½" F square on the diagonal of twelve 1½" x 2½" D rectangles. Note angle. Trim and press toward the triangle.

12. Reverse the angle and sew 1½" F squares on the remaining twelve D rectangles. Trim and press toward the triangle.

13. Sew one pieced rectangle to each side of an X square. Note orientation. Make 12 (2½" x 4½").

14. Sew one section to two opposite sides of the center square. Make 3 (4½" x 8½").

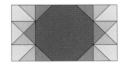

15. Sew a 2½" D square to the end of the remaining sections. Make 6 (2½" x 8½").

16. Sew one to the top and bottom of each block. Press.

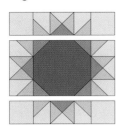

17. Prepare a bias strip for the stem and cut the leaves. Pin the stem and leaves to the 8½" x 10½" D rectangle in a pleasing manner. Appliqué pieces by machine or by hand with matching thread. Sew the two sections together. You may wish to insert the stem under a triangle petal by taking out a stitch or two and inserting the stem in the seam. Several hand stitches will hold it in place. Embellish as you wish.

18. Sew a 12½" elongated checkerboard strip to the top of one sunflower and the bottom of a second. Sew a 3½" x 8½" C strip to the top and bottom of the third sunflower (8½" x 22½").

Cutting

From the tan sashing fabric C:
  2: 2½" x 64½" sashing strips
  2: 6½" x 64½" sashing strips

From the floral border fabric A:
  4: 8½" x 48½" border strips
  8: 6½" x 8½" rectangles
  4: 8½" squares

From the green border print B:
  4: 6½" x 64½" border strips
  8: 8½" squares
  4: 6½" squares
  16: 4½" squares

From the medium green print K:
  32: 4½" squares
  16: 3½" squares

Sashing

1. Sew blocks together in strips using the diagram as guide. Each strip should measure 64½" long.

2. Sew C sashing strips and blocks together. Press toward sashing (64½" x 64½").

Side Borders

1. Sew a 4½" K square on the diagonal to opposite corners of an 8½" B square. Repeat on the remaining corners. Make 8 (8½" x 8½").

2. Sew one square to each end of border A.

3. Sew borders A and B together on long sides. Press toward B. (16½" x 64½")

4. Sew one border strip to each side of the quilt.

Corner Blocks

1. Sew a 3½" K square on the diagonal to opposite corners of a 6½" B square. Repeat on the remaining corners. Make 4 (6½" x 6½").

2. Sew a 6½" x 8½" A rectangle to each square. Make 4 (14½" x 6½").

3. Sew a 4½" B square on the diagonal to opposite corners of an 8½" A square. Repeat on the remaining corners. Make 4 (8½" x 8½").

4. Sew a 6½" x 8½" A rectangle to each square. Make 4 (8½" x 14½").

Borders

5. Sew pairs of blocks together as shown. Make 4 (14½" x 14½").

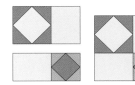

6. Sew a pieced square to each end of the remaining borders. Sew the borders to the top and bottom of the quilt (92½" x 92½").

The Garden Medley Sampler Quilt *also looks beautiful in other colorways.*

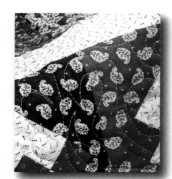

Happy Day Baby Quilt

This colorful baby quilt will brighten up the day of any child lucky enough to receive it. The nautical look of the red, white, and blue fabrics would also be ideal for a cottage throw or a picnic blanket.

Finished size 37½" x 47½"

Materials

- ⅛ yard red print
- ⅛ yard blue print
- 1¼ yards white print
- 5 (or more) fat quarters assorted red and blue prints

Cutting

From the red print:
  2: 1¾" x width of fabric (WOF)

From the blue print:
  1: 1¾" x WOF
  1: 1¾" x WOF, subcut into (1) 15" strip and (4) 1¾" squares (for corner blocks)

From the white print:
  3: 1¾" x WOF
  3: 3" x WOF, cut into (30) 3" squares
  2: 3½" x WOF (for sashing)
  4: 4¼" x WOF (for border)
  1: 1¾" x WOF, subcut into (1) 15" strip, and (8) 3" strips (for corner blocks)

From the assorted reds and blues:
  15 pairs 6½" squares, cut once on the diagonal
  2½" strips to equal 190" (for binding)

Directions

1. Following the directions on page 8, create five Four-Patch on Point #1 blocks with blue center squares and ten Four-Patch on Point blocks with red center squares. Use the assorted red and blue 6½" triangles to create the corners. (See page 121 for tips on centering.)

2. Line up the blocks in a pleasing arrangement, using the diagram as a model. The two outside vertical rows each have five red-centered Four-Patch blocks, while the inner vertical row has five blue-centered Four-Patch blocks. Sew each row together.

3. Lay out the pieced rows with the vertical sashing strips and borders. The two outer borders are 4¼" x 40½" and the two inner sashing strips are 3½" x 40½". Sew the vertical rows together (30½" x 40½"). Press toward the sashing strips and borders.

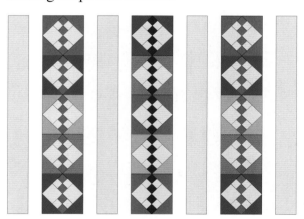

4. To create the corner blocks, layer the 15" blue and white strips right sides together and sew along the long edge. Press toward the blue. Cut into eight 1¾" sections.

5. Layer two sections together, matching opposing seams, to create a four-patch.

6. Attach one 3" white strip along the side of each four-patch. Sew one blue square to the end of each remaining 3" white strip. Attach to the top of each four-patch to create the corner blocks (4¼" x 4¼").

7. Cut the top and bottom border strips (4¼" x 30½") and using the diagram as a model, attach a corner block to each end. Press toward the border. Attach the top and bottom borders to the quilt (38" x 48").

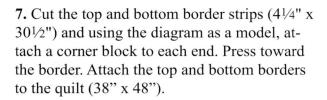

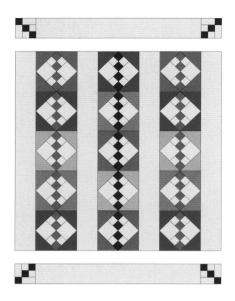

Finishing

1. Sandwich, quilt, and bind your quilt with 2½" wide binding strips pieced to measure 190". The quilt shown was quilted with an all-over whimsical design.

2. Sign and date your quilt.

Leftover blocks and fabric scraps can be combined to create a back that is nearly as much fun as the front!

Southern Comfort Lap Quilt

The blue and tan civil war reproduction fabrics lend a historic feel to this project. It's a perfect gift for the man in your life.

Finished size 52½" x 52½"

Materials

- 1½ yards tan plaid
- ½ yard white print
- ¼ yard tan with small stars
- ¼ yard navy hexagons
- ⅓ yard navy with blue flowers
- ⅔ yard brown
- ⅞ yard navy and tan floral

Cutting

From the tan plaid:
   12: 8½" squares (for setting squares)
   4: 6½" squares (for border)
   6: 2½" x width of fabric (WOF) (for binding)

From the white print:
   1: 1¾" x WOF
   20: 4½" squares

From the tan with stars:
   1: 1¾" x WOF
   8: 3" squares

From the navy hexagons:
   2: 1¾" x WOF
   8: 3" squares

From the navy floral:
   5: 8½" squares

From the brown print:
   16: 6½" squares, cut once on the diagonal

From the navy and tan floral:
   4: 6½" x 40½" navy and tan floral (for border)

Directions

1. Following the directions on page 8, create four Four-Patch on Point #1 blocks with white center squares and navy hexagons and four Four-Patch on Point blocks with navy hexagon center squares and tan with stars. Use the brown 6½" triangles to create the corners. (See page 121 for tips on centering.)

2. Following Step 3 for Corner blocks on page 22, create five Corner blocks with navy floral centers and white corners.

3. Using the diagram as a model, alternate Four-Patch on Point blocks with setting blocks and Corner blocks as shown. Note the orientation of each block. Assemble in rows of five blocks and join the rows to create the center square (40½" x 40½").

4. Attach the two side borders (6½" x 40½"). Press toward the borders.

5. Sew a 6½" tan plaid square to each end of the remaining borders. Press toward the border. Attach these to the top and bottom of the quilt (52½" x 52½").

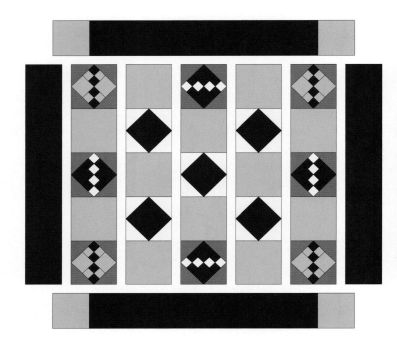

Finishing

1. Sandwich, quilt, and bind your quilt with 2½" wide binding strips pieced to measure 220". The quilt shown was quilted with small wreaths in the alternate and pieced blocks. There is echo quilting around the four-patches, and a wandering feather design fills the borders.

2. Sign and date your quilt.

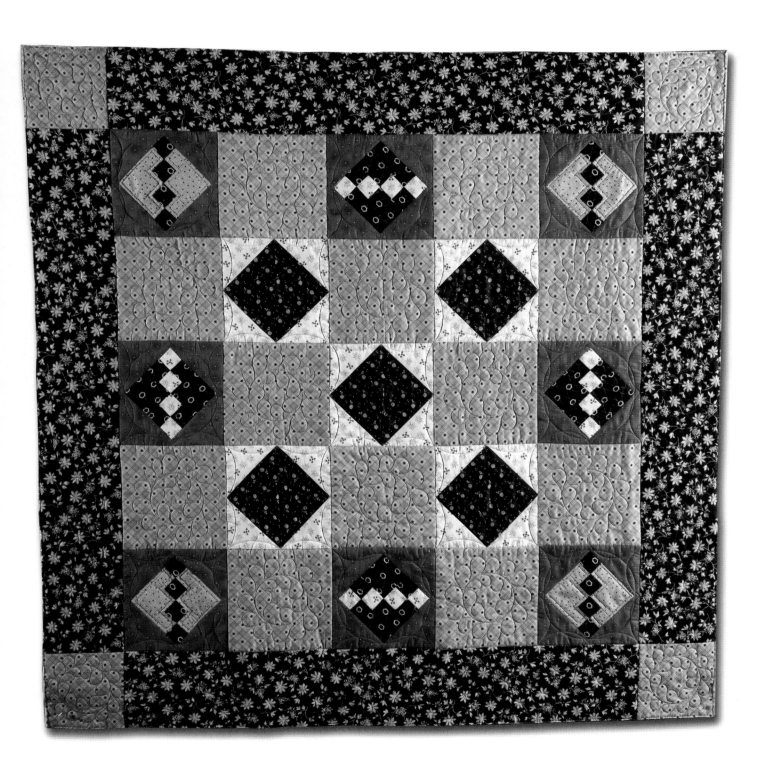

Cherry Basket Wall Quilt

This wall quilt also doubles as a table mat.
Make one to coordinate with your kitchen or breakfast nook.

Finished size 26" x 26"

Materials
- ½ yard cherry print
- ½ yard red
- ½ yard white print
- ⅛ yard green

Cutting
From the cherry print (A):
  2: 5" squares
  2: 2½" x 8½" strips
  1: 2½" x 18½" strip
  4: 3½" x 20" strips

From the red (B):
  14: 3" squares
  4: 3½" squares
  3: 2½" x width of fabric for binding
  2: 5" squares

From the white print (D):
  14: 3" squares
  8: 2½" x 4½" rectangles
  4: 2½" squares

From the green:
  2: 1¼" x 18½" strips
  2: 1¼" x 20" strips

Directions

1. Following Steps 1 – 11 on page 10, make four Basket blocks (8½" x 8½").

2. Referring to the diagram, arrange the blocks and sew the 2½" x 8½" sashing strips between the blocks to form horizontal rows. Add the center sashing strip (2½" x 18½"). Press toward the sashing strips (18½" x 18½").

3. Attach the inner green borders (1¼" x 18½") to both sides and then the top and bottom (1¼" x 20"). Press toward the borders.

4. Attach the cherry borders (3½" x 20") to each side. Press toward the cherry border. Sew the red squares to each end of the remaining borders. Press toward the cherry border. Attach the top and bottom borders to the quilt, nesting seams (26" x 26").

Finishing

1. Sandwich, quilt, and bind your quilt with 2½" wide binding strips pieced to measure 120". Our quilt was stippled in the white areas and echo quilted throughout the baskets. A chain design fills the borders with a medallion in each corner.

2. Sign and date your quilt.

Cherry Basket Table Runner

The large center section bordered by two blocks allows you to show off a favorite fabric.

Finished size 17" x 52½"

Materials
- ½ yard cherry print
- ¼ yard white
- ⅔ yard red
- ¼ yard green

Cutting
From the cherry print (A):
  1: 5" square
  1: 17" x 19" rectangle (for center piece)

From the white (D):
  7: 3" squares
  4: 2½" x 4½" rectangles
  2: 2½" squares

From the red (B):
  7: 3" squares
  1: 5" square
  2: 9½" squares, cut once on the diagonal
  4: 2½" x WOF (for binding)

From the green:
  4: 2½" x 8½" strips
  4: 2½" x 12½" strips

Directions

1. Following Steps 1-11 on page 10, make two Basket blocks.

2. Attach first the top and bottom green sashing strips and then the side sashings (12½" x 12½").

3. Center two red triangles on the "top" of each basket. (See page 121 for tips on centering.)

4. Sew one basket piece to each end of the cherry rectangle. Press toward the cherry center.

Finishing

1. Sandwich, quilt, and bind your quilt with 2½" wide binding strips pieced to measure 140". In our example, the baskets were stitched in the ditch with a wave design in the green sashing. The center was crosshatched.

2. Sign and date your quilt.

Together with the matching wall quilt (page 34), this set makes an ideal gift for your favorite hostess!

Vintage Baskets

This quilt combines appliquéd handle baskets with strategically colored Corner blocks to create the large center star.

Finished size 34" x 34"

Materials
- ½ yard each of three black prints
- ⅔ yard tan
- ⅓ yard rust
- ¾ yard gold
- ½ yard black border print

Cutting
From each of the three black prints (F):
  1: 6½" square, cut once diagonally
  1: 5¼" square, cut twice diagonally
  2: 1½" x 15" bias strips

From the tan (D):
  3: 5¼" squares, cut twice diagonally
  4: 8½" x 8½" squares
  5: 4½" x 8½"

From the rust:
  8: 4½" x 4½"
  4: 4" x 4" (for border squares)

From the gold:
  8: 4½" x 4½" squares.
  2: 2" x 24½" (for inner borders)
  2: 2" x 27½" (for inner borders)
  4: 2½" x WOF for binding

From the black border print:
  4: 4" x 27½" (for outer borders)

Directions

1. Following Steps 1 – 10 on page 11, make five Basket blocks with Appliqué Handles (8½" x 8½"). (For tips on making the bias handles, see page 123.)

2. Following Step 3 on page 22, make four Corner blocks with rust and gold corners. Note the orientation of the colors (8½" x 8½").

3. Arrange the baskets and corner blocks in horizontal rows (8½" x 24½"). Sew the rows together (24½" x 24½").

4. Sew the inner gold borders to the sides and then the top and bottom of the quilt (27½" x 27½").

5. Sew a black border to each side of the quilt. Sew a rust square to each end of remaining black borders. Attach to the top and bottom of the quilt. (34" x 34").

Finishing

1. Sandwich, quilt, and bind your quilt with 2½" wide binding strips pieced to measure 150". The example shown features McTavishing behind each of the baskets and feathered wreaths in the alternate blocks. All of the triangles are echo quilted.

2. Sign and date your quilt.

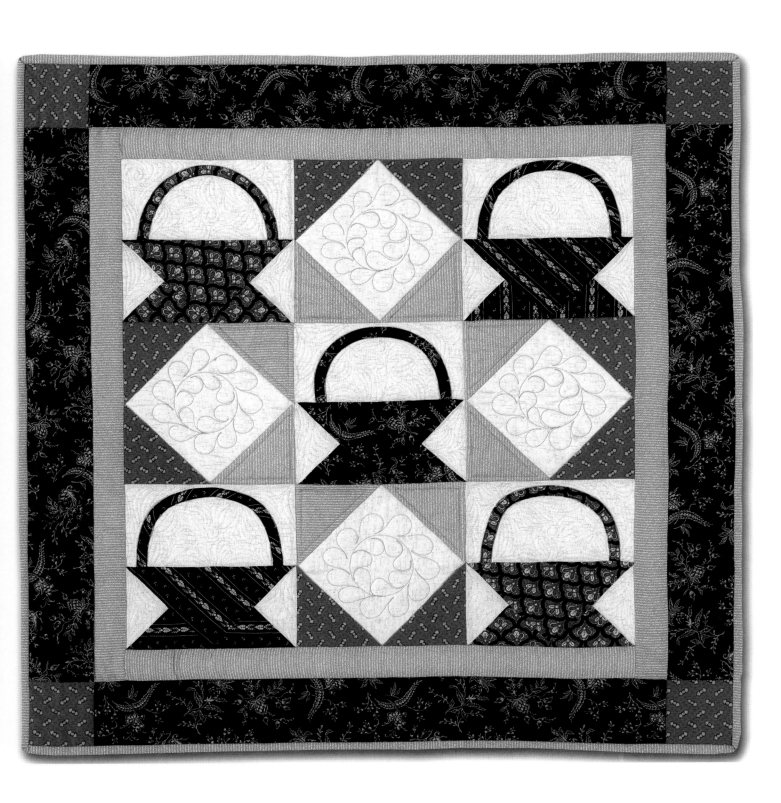

Primitive Red Baskets

The simplicity of the red baskets against a muslin background lends an Amish look to this long wall hanging. An eye-catching centerpiece for any mantle.

Finished size 20½" x 62"

Materials
- ½ yard each of five assorted red prints
- ¼ yard red for inner border
- 2 yards muslin (cut borders first lengthwise)

Cutting
From each of the assorted reds (F):
  1: 6½" square red, cut once diagonally
  1: 5¼" square red, cut twice diagonally
  1: 1½ x 15" strip, cut on the bias

From the muslin (D):
  5: 4½" x 8½" muslin
  3: 5¼" squares muslin, cut twice diagonally
  6: 3" x 8½" muslin (for sashings)
  2: 3" x 55½" (for first border)
  2: 3" x 15½" (for outer border)
  2: 3" x 62" (for outer border)

From the inner border red:
  2: 1¼" x 13½"
  3: 1¼" x width of fabric

Directions
1. Following Steps 1 – 10 on page 11, create five Baskets with Appliquéd Handles. (You will have leftover red pieces.)

2. Referring to the diagram, alternate 8½" sashing strips with the baskets to create a long vertical strip. Add the top and bottom muslin first borders (13½" x 55½")

3. Sew the three 1¼" x WOF red inner border strips together end-to-end, and then sub-cut them into two 1¼" x 57" pieces.

4. Attach the red inner border, sides first and then top and bottom (15½" x 57").

5. Add the outer border sides and then top and bottom (20½" x 62").

Finishing

1. Sandwich, quilt, and bind your quilt with 2½" wide binding strips pieced to measure 180". Our quilt was stunningly quilted with McTavishing surrounding the baskets, which were echo quilted on the inside. A continuous vine appears in the outer border.

2. Sign and date your quilt.

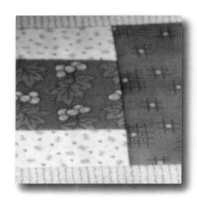

Log Cabin Placemats

Quick, easy, and versatile, these elongated log cabin placemats can be made to fit any décor or color scheme.

Finished size 12" x 16"

Materials
- Fat quarters or scraps of three lights
- Fat quarters or scraps of three darks
- Scraps for center fabric
- ½ yard heavy fabric for backing

Cutting
For one placemat #1:
  1: 2½" x 3½" center
  2: 1½" x 3½" light #1
  2: 1½" x 6½" light #2
  2: 1½" x 9½" light #3
  2: 2" x 4½" dark #1
  2: 2" x 6½" dark #2
  2: 2" x 8½" dark #3

  2: 2½" x 12½" border
  2: 2½" x 8½" border
  4: 2½" squares for cornerstones
  1: 15" x 18" backing

For one placemat #2:
  1: 2½" x 3½" center
  2: 1½" x 3½" dark #1
  2: 1½" x 6½" dark #2
  2: 1½" x 9½" dark #3
  2: 2" x 4½" light #1
  2: 2" x 6½" light #2
  2: 2" x 8½" light #3
  2: 2½" x 12½" border
  2: 2½" x 8½" border
  4: 2½" squares for cornerstones
  1: 15" x 18" backing

Directions

1. Follow the directions for Log Cabin #1 on page 12 or Log Cabin #2 on page 13.

2. Sew the 2½" x 12½" borders to the top and bottom. Attach the 2½" cornerstones to each end of the remaining borders. Sew the side borders to the placemat.

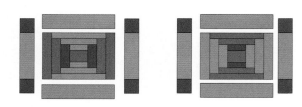

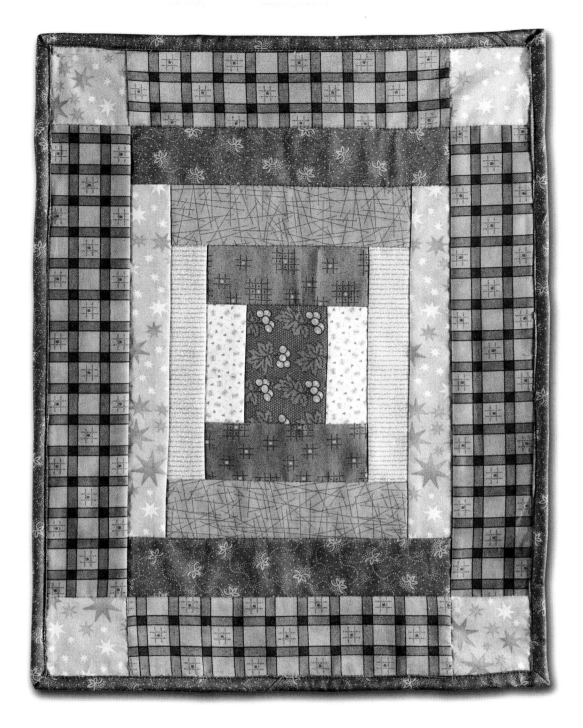

Finishing

Follow the instructions at right for making and finishing the placemats or sandwich, quilt, and bind them with 2½" wide binding strips pieced to measure 70".

Making Placemats

For a quick and easy finish to your placemats, use a heavy backing fabric and quilt as you go. Starting in the center, place the center fabric right-side up with the next piece placed on top of it right-side down. Stitch your seam as usual through all layers. Press away from the center. Add each subsequent piece in the same manner. Bind to finish.

Clover Patch Quilt

Gather up a collection of coordinating prints —
plaids, florals, stripes — and showcase them in this simple set.

Finished size 68½" x 84½"

Materials
- ⅓ yard of 12 colors
- ⅓ yard of 12 backgrounds
- 2 yards sage green
- ⅔ yard binding fabric

Cutting
From each of the 12 colors (H/I):
　5: 3" squares, cut once on the diagonal
　1: 4½" square
　1: 5" square, cut once on the diagonal
　1: 2½" x 10" rectangle
　1: 2½" square

From each of the 12 backgrounds (D):
　6: 3" squares, cut once on the diagonal
　2: 7" squares, cut once on the diagonal

From the sage green:
　15: 4½" x 12½" strips
　6: 8½" x 68½" strips

From the binding fabric:
　8: 2½" x width of fabric

Directions

1. Following Steps 1 – 13 on page 14 make twelve Clover blocks. Each block will only use two fabrics: the background and the focus fabric (12½" x 12½").

2. Sew five sashing strips and four blocks together to create a vertical row. Make 3 (12½" x 68½").

3. Alternate block rows with 4½" x 68½" sashing strips. Sew together (68½ x 68½").

4. Sew the top and bottom borders to the quilt (68½" x 84½").

Finishing

1. Sandwich, quilt, and bind your quilt with 2½" wide binding strips pieced to measure 320". In our example, the blocks are stippled in matching thread, and feathered scrolls fill the sashings and borders.

2. Sign and date your quilt.

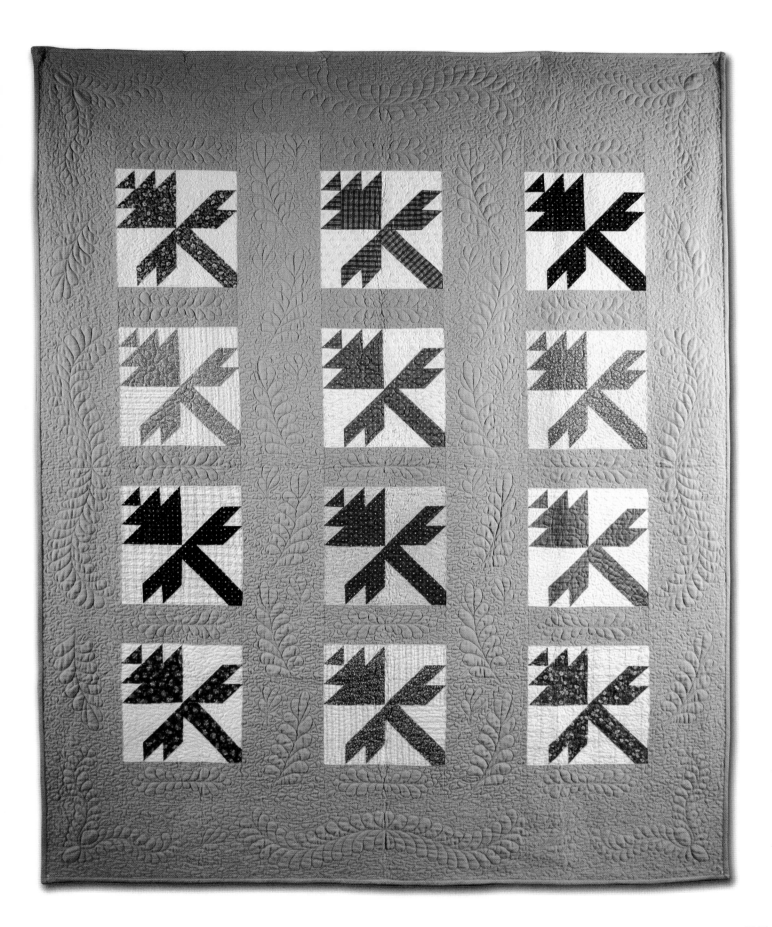

Clover Pillow

A leftover block set on point makes a quick companion project to any quilt.

Finished size 22" x 22"

Materials
- ¼ yard red
- ¼ yard medium blue
- ¼ yard cream
- ⅓ yard plaid
- 1⅓ yard red paisley

Cutting

From the red (H):
  5: 3" squares, cut once on the diagonal
  1: 2½" x 10" strip
  1: 2½" square

From the blue (I):
  1: 4½" square
  1: 5" square, cut once on the diagonal

From the cream (D):
  2: 7" squares, cut once on the diagonal
  6: 3" squares, cut once on the diagonal

From the plaid:
  2: 9½" squares, cut once on the diagonal

From the paisley:
  2: 22¼" x 26" rectangles (for pillow back)
  2: 3" x 17¼" strips
  2: 3" x 22¼" strips

Directions

1. Following steps 1 – 13 on page 14, make one Clover block.

2. Center a plaid triangle on each of the four sides of the block. (See page 121 for tips on centering.) Press toward the triangles. Trim to 17¼" x 17¼".

13. Attach the red paisley side borders and then the top and bottom borders (22¼" x 22¼").

Finishing

1. Sandwich and quilt your pillow top as desired. The pillow shown was stippled in the cream areas and echo quilted throughout the inside of the clover.

2. Follow the instructions on page 123 for finishing pillows. Add a flange by stitching in the ditch where the paisley border meets the plaid triangles.

Antique Blue Quilt

This antique blue and white quilt is a variation of our Clover block.
Watch the position of your half-square triangles in the blossom!

Finished size 80½" x 90½"

Materials
• 1½ yards blue
• 7½ yards white

Cutting
From the blue:
    64: 3" squares, cut once on the diagonal
    16: 4½" square
    16: 5" square, cut once on the diagonal
    16: 2½" x 10" rectangle
    16: 2½" square

From the white:
    2: 11½" x 68½", cut lengthwise (for borders)*

    2: 6½" x 90½", cut lengthwise (for borders)*
    80: 3" squares, cut once on the diagonal
    32: 7" squares, cut once on the diagonal
    16: 2½" square
    9: 12½" squares
    3: 18" x 18" squares, cut twice on the diagonal
    2: 11" squares, cut once on the diagonal
    9: 2½" x width of fabric (for binding)

*Note: If you prefer to have borders without seams, cut them first, lengthwise. You can also cut them crosswise and piece them together.

Directions

1. Using the 3" blue and white triangles, make 128 half-square triangles. Trim to 2½" x 2½".

2. Sew the half-square triangles together in pairs as shown. Note orientation. Make 32 of each orientation (2½" x 4½").

3. Sew one set of triangle squares to the top of the 4½" blue square. Note orientation. Make 16 (4½" x 6½").

4. Sew a 2½" white square to the top of 16 of the triangle square sets. Note orientation. Sew this piece to the adjacent side of the 4½" square set. Make 16 (6½" x 6½").

5. Sew a 3" white triangle to the end of a triangle square set. Note orientation. Sew this set to the 5" blue triangle and attach to the 7" white triangle as shown. Make 16 (6½" x 6½").

6. Sew a 3" white triangle to the end of a triangle square set. Note orientation. Sew this set to the 5" blue triangle and attach to the 7" white triangle as shown. Make 16 (6½" x 6½").

7. To make stem, center and sew a 2½" x 10" blue strip between two 7" white triangles. Make 16. Trim to 6½" x 6½". Sew a 2½" blue square on the diagonal at the bottom of the stem.

8. Arrange the squares and sew together in pairs. Sew the pairs together to create the Antique Blue block.

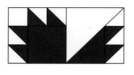

9. Arrange and sew blocks, setting squares, and setting triangles in diagonal rows. Sew rows together. The setting triangles are cut generously. Trim leaving a ¼" seam allowance (68½" x 68½").

10. Sew borders to the top and bottom (68½" x 90½") and then to each side of the quilt (80½" x 90½").

Finishing

1. Sandwich, quilt, and bind your quilt with 2½" wide binding strips pieced to measure 360". This antique quilt was hand quilted with an allover clamshell design.

2. Sign and date your quilt.

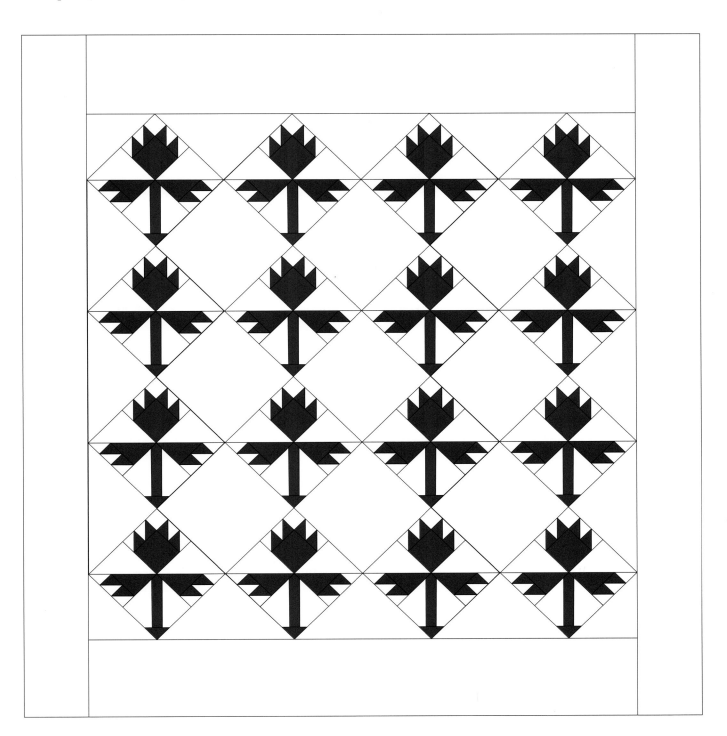

Stars in the Window

The red and green stars glittering through the gold windows give a holiday feel to this quilt. It would look lovely in scrappy blues too.

Finished size 44" x 49½"

Materials
- ⅞ yard gold
- ⅓ yard red
- ⅓ yard green
- 1 yard green paisley
- ⅔ yard light
- ⅓ yard tan print
- 1¼ yard gold stripe

Cutting
From the gold (A):
   12: 1½" x 4"
   2: 2¼" x 28" (for the inner border)
   2: 2¼" x 35½" (for the inner border)
   5: 2½" x width of fabric (for binding)

From the red (K):
   8: 2¼" x 4" rectangles
   48: 2¼" squares

From the green (K):
   8: 2¼" x 4" rectangles
   48: 2¼" squares

From the paisley (K):
   4: 2¼" x 4" rectangles
   2: 5¾" x 28" (for outer borders)
   2: 6¾" x 35½" (for outer borders)

From the light (D):
   24: 2¼" x 4" rectangles
   24: 2¼" x 5" rectangles
   48: 2¼" squares

From the tan print:
   7: 8½" x 5½" (for the alternate blocks)

From the gold stripe:
   14: 1½" x 8½" (for the horizontal sashings)
   2: 2¼" x 35½" (for the vertical sashings)

Directions

1. Following the directions on page 16, create six red-pointed stars (two with paisley centers, four with red centers) and six green-pointed stars (two with paisley centers, four with green centers). All stars will have a gold strip in the center.

2. Referring to the diagram, alternate stars with horizontal sashing strips and alternate blocks to form three vertical rows. Press toward the sashing strips (8½" x 35½").

3. Attach the two vertical 2¼" sashing strips to both sides of the center row. Press toward the sashing strips (12" x 35½").

4. Sew the gold inner border pieces to their coordinating outer border pieces to form four border strips (7½" x 28" and 8½" x 35½").

5. Attach the side border pieces to the quilt center. Press toward the border.

6. Sew a star block to each end of the remaining two border pieces. Note the color placement. Press toward the border. Attach the top and bottom borders to the quilt (44" x 49½").

Finishing

1. Sandwich, quilt, and bind your quilt with 2½" wide binding strips pieced to measure 200". Our quilt features echo quilting around the stars and feathered scrolls in the alternate blocks. More feathered scroll designs complete the border.

2. Sign and date your quilt.

Cutting Striped Sashings and Borders

If you are planning on piecing the striped sashings as shown, you will need all of your stripes running vertically. This means that you have to cut the long sections first and then use the leftover fabric for your shorter sections. (Cut the vertical sashings first horizontally, and then cut the horizontal sashings vertically!) Choose the same place in the stripe to cut all of your pieces so that the stripe is consistent throughout the quilt.

Our Stars in the Window *has a Christmas feel because of the fabrics chosen.*
You could easily make a Flowers in the Window *quilt by choosing alternate colors.*

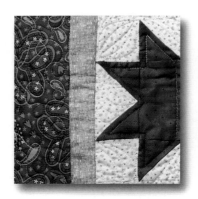

Star Lily Wall Quilt

Stars become flowers in this small charmer.
These lilies will brighten your home all year long.

Finished size 29½" x 38½"

Materials
- Fat quarter of three blue fabrics
- 1 yard background
- ⅓ yard gold
- ½ yard paisley
- ⅓ yard binding
- ½ yard green for stems
- Scraps for leaves

Cutting
From each of the blue (K):
  2: 2¼" x 4" rectangles
  8: 2¼" squares

From the background (D):
  6: 2¼" x 4" rectangles
  6: 2¼" x 5" rectangles
  12: 2¼" squares

  2: 3½" x 7½"
  1: 3½" x 8½"
  1: 3½" x 11½"
  1: 8½" x 7½"
  1: 19½" x 11½"

From the green:
  3: 1½" x 25" bias strips

From the gold (A):
  3: 1½" x 4" rectangles
  2: 2" x 22½" strips
  2: 2" x 28½" strips

From the paisley:
  2: 4" x 29½" strips
  2: 4" x 31½" strips

From the binding fabric:
  4: 2½" x width of fabric

Directions

1. Following Steps 1 – 8 on page 16, make three Star Lily blocks (8½" x 7½").

2. Following the diagram, arrange and sew the quilt top.

3. Using the bias strip technique (page 123), fashion three 25" bias stems. Arrange and appliqué leaves and stems in a pleasing manner. (See tip box on this page).

4. Sew the inner borders to each side and then to the top and bottom (22½" x 31½").

5. Sew the outer borders to each side and then to the top and bottom of the quilt (29½" x 38½").

Finishing

1. Sandwich, quilt, and bind your quilt with 2½" wide binding strips pieced to measure 150". Our flowers were echo quilted with McTavishing throughout the background.

2. Sign and date your quilt.

Making stems and leaves

Bias strips are ideal for stems (and basket handles) because they are flexible and can be formed to any shape. This method also provides finished edges. Freeform leaves can be cut from scraps and appliquéd to your project with your favorite appliqué method: needle turn, raw edge, freezer paper.

1930s Twister

The yellow fabric found in the centers and repeated in the borders gives this quilt sparkle! The cheery 1930s fabrics would make this a good choice for a new baby.

Finished size 44" x 44".

Materials
- Fat quarter of nine assorted 1930s prints
- 1¼ yards white
- 1 yard yellow
- Fat quarter green
- Scraps of pink

Cutting

From each of the 1930s prints (H):
 4: 3½" squares, cut once on the diagonal

From the white (D):
 36: 3½" squares, cut once on the diagonal
 8: 3¼" squares, cut once on the diagonal

 24: 2¾" x 8" rectangles
 2: 3" squares (for corner blocks in inner border)
 4: 4½" x 36" (for outer border)
 2: 5" squares (for corner blocks in outer border)

From the yellow (J):
 9: 3" squares
 4: 2½" x 32" (for inner border)
 2: 5" squares (for corner blocks in outer border)
 5: 2½" x WOF (for binding)

From the green (K):
 8: 3¼" squares, cut once on the diagonal

From the pink scraps:
 2: 3" squares (for corner blocks in inner border)

Directions

1. Following Steps 1 – 4 on page 17, assemble nine Twister blocks (8" x 8").

2. Add top and bottom sashings (2¾" x 8") to six blocks. These blocks will be used in the top and bottom rows of the quilt.

3. Using the 3¼" green and white triangles, create 16 half-square triangles. Trim to 2¾". Sew one half-square triangle to each end of 8 sashing strips (2¾" x 12½"). Note orientation.

4. Lay out the blocks with the sashing strips. The top and bottom rows have pieced sashings and the middle row has plain sashings. Sew the rows together to create the center of the quilt (32" x 32").

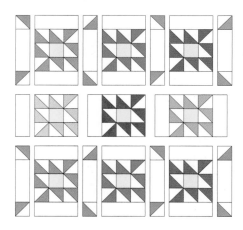

5. Using the pink and white 3" triangles, create half-square triangles. Make 4. Trim to 2½".

6. Sew the yellow inner borders to each side of the quilt. Sew a pink/white half-square triangle to each end of the remaining inner borders. Attach these to the top and bottom of the quilt (36" x 36").

7. Using the 5" yellow and white triangles, create half-square triangles. Make 4. Trim to 4½".

8. Sew the white outer borders to each side of the quilt. Sew a yellow/white half-square triangle to each end of the remaining outer borders. Attach these to the top and bottom of the quilt (44" x 44").

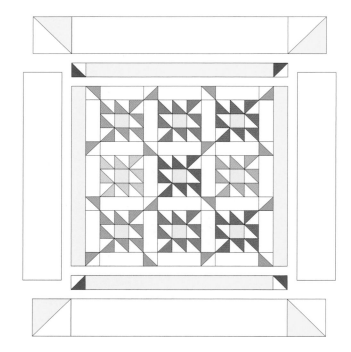

Finishing

1. Sandwich, quilt, and bind your quilt with 2½" wide binding strips pieced to measure 190". The center of each Twister block was quilted with a leaf medallion and there is meandering in the white areas. The yellow inner border has a repeating teardrop design, and the outer borders contain a feather design.

2. Sign and date your quilt.

Civil War Twister

By arranging these blocks on point, you get an entirely different look from the previous quilt. This project is an ideal showcase for your reproduction fabrics.

Finished size 41½" x 41½"

Materials
- Scraps of five assorted browns
- ⅓ yard pink
- ⅔ yard cream
- 1 yard pink and brown paisley
- ⅝ yard brown border print

Cutting

From each of the assorted browns (H):
  4: 3½" squares, cut once on the diagonal

From the pink (J):
  4: 3¼" squares, cut once on the diagonal
  5: 3" squares
  2: 1½" x 31½" strips (for inner border)
  2: 1½" x 33½" strips (for inner border)

From the cream (D):
  20: 3½" squares, cut once on the diagonal
  6: 3¼" squares, cut once on the diagonal
  16: 2¾" x 8" strips

From the paisley:
  2: 3¼" squares
  1: 16" square, cut twice on the diagonal (for setting triangles)
  2: 10" squares, cut once on the diagonal (for corners)
  4: 4½" squares
  5: 2½" x width of fabric (for binding)

From the brown border print:
  4: 4½" x 33½" strips

Directions

1. Following Steps 1 – 4 on page 17, create five brown Twister blocks with pink centers.

2. Sew a cream sashing strip to the top of two of the Twister blocks. Sew a cream sashing strip to both the top and the bottom of the remaining three Twister blocks.

3. Sew together the 3¼" cream and pink triangles to form half-square triangles. Make 8. Trim to 2¾" x 2¾". Sew a triangle square to one end of a cream sashing strip. Make 2 of each orientation.

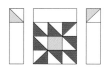

4. Arrange setting triangles, sashing strips and a Twister block to form the outer rows. Make 2.

5. Sew together the 3¼" cream and paisley triangles to form half-square triangles. Make 4. Trim to 2¾" x 2¾". Sew a triangle square to each end of a cream sashing strip. Note orientation. Make 2.

6. Sew the remaining pink/cream triangle squares to each end of a sashing strip. Make 2.

7. Following the diagram, arrange and sew the center row.

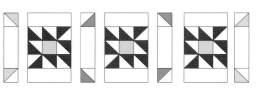

8. Sew the top and bottom rows to the center row. Note: Sew with the center row on top to avoid stretching the biases.

9. Center the corner triangles to finish the center quilt square. (See page 121 for tips on centering). Add the pink inner border, attaching sides (1½" x 31½") and then the top and bottom (1½" x 33½").

10. Attach the brown outer borders to either side. Press toward the border. Sew the paisley squares to each end of the two remaining border strips. Press toward the border. Attach these to the top and bottom of the quilt (41½" x 41½").

Finishing

1. Sandwich, quilt, and bind your quilt with 2½" wide binding strips pieced to measure 180". Our quilt features stippling in the cream areas, straight line echo quilting in the setting triangles, and a feather design throughout the outer border.

2. Sign and date your quilt.

Make a quick and easy pillow using an extra block and the directions on page 123.

Christmas Twister Table Runner

Only three blocks are needed for this holiday centerpiece.
Make it in Spring colors for your Easter table.

Finished size 17½" x 50"

Materials
• Fat quarter or scraps green
• Fat quarter or scraps red
• ⅜ yard beige
• Fat quarter or scraps gold
• ⅔ yard Christmas print

Cutting

From the green (H):
    4: 3½" squares, cut once on the diagonal

From the red (H):
    8: 3½" squares, cut once on the diagonal

From the beige (D):
    12: 3½" squares, cut once on the diagonal
    10: 2¾" x 8" rectangles
    4: 3¼" squares, cut once on the diagonal

From the gold (J/K):
    3: 3" squares
    4: 3¼" squares, cut once on the diagonal

From the Christmas print:
    2: 3" x 32" strips
    1: 13" square, cut once on the diagonal

Directions

1. Following Steps 1 – 4 on page 17, assemble three Twister blocks (8" x 8").

2. Sew a top and bottom sashing strip to each block (8" x 12½").

3. Sew the 3¼" beige and gold triangles together to make half-square triangles. Make 8. Trim to 2¾" x 2¾". Sew one to each end of the remaining sashing strips. Note orientation. Make 4 (2¾" x 12½").

4. Alternate sashings and blocks and sew together. Attach the long border strips to the top and bottom of the centerpiece.

5. Center a Christmas print triangle on either end. (See page 121 for tips on centering.)

Finishing

1. Sandwich, quilt, and bind your table runner with 2½" wide binding strips pieced to measure 130". The quilt shown has stippling in the sashings and a free form echo design in each block.

2. Sign and date your table runner.

Puzzle Table Mat

This small table topper is ideal for the top of a dresser or bedside table next to your Garden Medley Sampler Quilt.

Finished size 12½" x 24½"

Materials
- Fat quarter medium green
- Fat quarter blue
- Fat quarter red
- Fat quarter white
- ¼ yard yellow plaid

Cutting
From the medium green (K):
   6: 2½" squares
   6: 2½" x 4½" rectangles

From the blue (I):
   6: 2½" squares
   6: 2½" x 4½" rectangles

From the red (H):
   6: 2½" squares
   6: 2½" x 4½" rectangles

From the white (D):
   6: 2½" squares
   6: 2½" x 4½" rectangles

From the yellow plaid:
   3: 2½" x width of fabric
   (for binding)

Directions

1. Following steps 1 – 6 on page 18, make three Puzzle blocks (8½" x 12½").

2. Sew the three Puzzle blocks together to create the table mat (12½" x 24½").

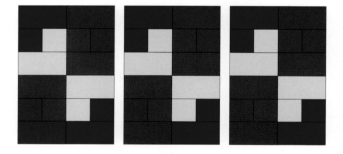

Finishing

1. Sandwich, quilt, and bind your quilt with 2½" wide binding strips pieced to measure 90". Our quilt was stippled in the light and green areas and echo quilted in the blue and red areas.

2. Sign and date your quilt.

The Puzzle Table Mat *doubles as an easy wall hanging*

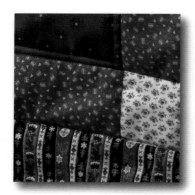

Garden Maze Table Runner

Although this project uses the same block as the previous one, it only uses two fabrics, which actually makes the design seem more complex. It reminds me of one of those garden mazes ... follow the diagrams closely so you don't get lost!

Finished size 22½" x 38½"

Materials
- ¼ yard brown
- ⅓ yard white
- ¾ yard rust
- ⅓ yard stripe

Cutting

From the brown (K/H):
  12: 2½" x 4½" rectangles
  1: 2½" x width of fabric (WOF)

From the white (D/I):
  12: 2½" x 4½" rectangles
  1: 2½" x WOF
  8: 2½" squares

From the rust:
  4: 2½" x 12½" strips
  6: 2½" x 8½" strips
  4: 3½" squares
  4: 2½" x WOF (for binding)

From the stripe:
  2: 3½" x 32½" strips
  2: 3½" x 16½" strips

Directions

1. Sew the 2½" white and brown strips together lengthwise and subcut into twelve 2½" x 4½" pieces.

2. Center a pieced section between 2½" x 4½" white and brown strips. Note orientation. Make 6 (4½" x 6½").

3. Center a pieced section between 2½" x 4½" white and brown strips. Note orientation. Make 6 (4½" x 6½").

4. Sew a block from Step 2 to a block from Step 3. Note orientation. Make 6 (6½" x 8½").

5. Sew blocks together in pairs to create 3 Puzzle blocks (8½" x 12½").

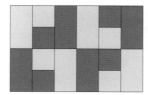

6. Attach rust 2½" x 8½" side sashings to each block. Press toward the sashing (8½" x 16½").

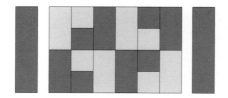

7. Sew a white 2½" square to each end of the 2½" x 12½" rust sashing strips. Press toward the rust sashing. Alternate pieced sashing strips with the blocks and sew together (16½" x 32½").

8. Attach the striped borders to either side of the quilt. Press toward the striped border. Sew a 3½" rust square to each end of the remaining striped borders. Press toward the striped border. Attach these to the top and bottom of the quilt (22½" x 38½").

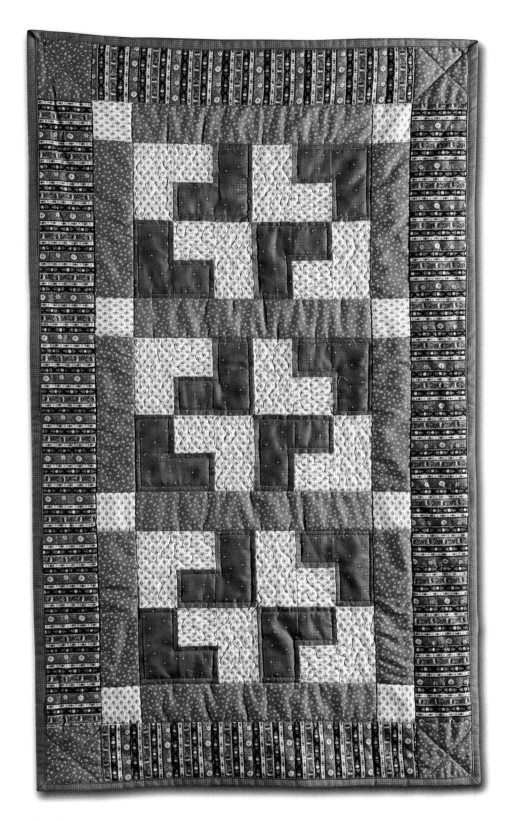

Finishing

1. Sandwich, quilt, and bind your quilt with 2½" wide binding strips pieced to measure 140". Our blocks were echo quilted in the dark and stippled in the light. The sashings and borders were stitched in the ditch.

2. Sign and date your quilt.

Hopscotch Baby Quilt

Simple four-patches combine to become larger blocks in this charming baby quilt. A good beginner's project.

Finished size 44½" x 44½"

Materials
- ⅝ yard light
- ⅝ yard medium green
- 1¼ yard yellow
- ½ yard dark green

Cutting
From the light (E):
   7: 2½" x width of fabric

From the medium green (G):
   7: 2½" x width of fabric

From the yellow:
   12: 4½" x 12½" strips
   4: 4½" x 36½" strips

From the dark green:
   5: 2½" x width of fabric
   (for binding)

Directions

1. Following Steps 1 – 2 on page 19, make 98 cuts (2½" x 4½").

2. Sew two cuts together to make four-patches. Make 49 (4½" x 4½").

3. Arrange 9 four-patches in three rows as shown. Sew the rows together to create a 36-patch. Make 4 (12½" x 12½").

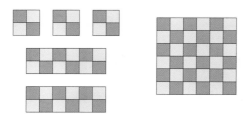

4. Alternate 36-patch blocks with 4½" x 12½" sashing strips to make two horizontal rows.

5. Alternate three four-patch blocks with two 4½" x 12½" sashing strips to create the horizontal inner border. Make 3 (4½" x 36½").

6. Alternate the horizontal inner borders with the 36-patch rows to create the quilt center (36½" x 36½").

7. Sew a 4½" x 36½" border to each side of the quilt center. Attach a four-patch to each end of the remaining borders. Sew the top and bottom borders to the quilt (44½" x 44½").

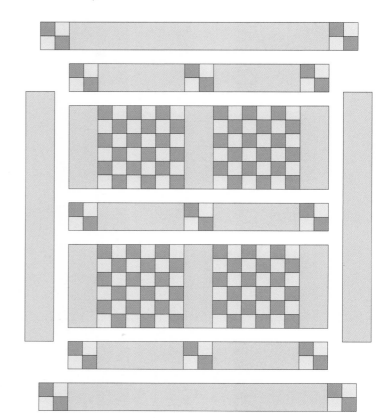

Finishing

1. Sandwich, quilt, and bind your quilt with 2½" wide binding strips pieced to measure 190". Our quilt features feathered scrolls in the sashings and borders with a free form echo design in the blocks.

2. Sign and date your quilt.

Checkerboard Pillow

A perfect complement to any project!
Use coordinating fabrics to create this accent piece.

Finished size 19" x 19"

Materials
- 1 yard red
- ⅛ yard green
- ⅛ yard tan
- ⅛ yard light
- ⅛ yard yellow

Cutting
From the red:
   1: 2½" x width of fabric (WOF)
   2: 3" x 14" strips
   2: 3" x 19" strips
   2: 24" x 19" (for pillow back)

From the green:
   1: 2½" x WOF

From the tan:
   1: 2½" x WOF

From the light:
   1: 2½" x WOF

From the yellow:
   2: 1¼" x 12½" strips
   2: 1¼" x 14" strips

Directions

1. Following Steps 1 – 2 on page 19, sew the red and light strips together and subcut to create 10 red/light segments. Sew together in pairs to create 5 four-patches (4½" x 4½").

2. Following Steps 1 – 2 on page 19, sew the green and tan strips together and subcut to create 8 green/tan segments. Sew together in pairs to create 4 four-patches (4½" x 4½").

3. Alternate two red with one green four-patch to create a row. Make 2 (4½" x 12½").

4. Alternate two green with one red four-patch to create a row. Make 1 (4½" x 12½").

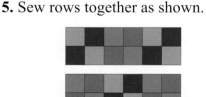

5. Sew rows together as shown.

6. Sew the light inner border to both sides and then the top and bottom (14" x 14").

7. Sew the red outer border to both sides and then the top and bottom (19" x 19").

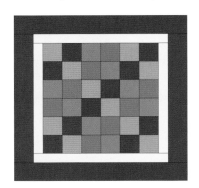

Finishing

1. Sandwich and quilt your pillow top as desired. The pillow shown was quilted with diagonal straight lines.

2. Follow the instructions on page 123 for finishing pillows.

Stellar Delight

With a simple change of color, sunflowers become stars.
Traditional blue and white is always a favorite color combination.

Finished size 34" x 34"

Materials
- ½ yard blue
- 1¾ yard white

Cutting
From the blue:
  4: 4½" squares
  8: 3¼" squares
  32: 1½" squares
  2: 1½" x 24" strips
  2: 1½" x 26" strips

From the white:
  16: 1½" squares
  8: 3¼" squares
  32: 1½" x 2½"
  16: 2½" squares
  1: 8½" square
  1: 14" square, cut twice on the diagonal
  2: 6½" x 6½" squares, cut once on the diagonal
  2: 4½" x 26" strips
  2: 4½" x 34" strips
  4: 2½" x width of fabric (for binding)

Directions

1. Following Steps 1 – 16 on pages 20 and 21, create four Sunflower blocks (8½" x 8½").

2. Arrange and sew blocks, setting squares, and setting triangles in diagonal rows. Sew rows together. The setting triangles are cut generously. Trim leaving a ¼" seam allowance (24" x 24").

3. Attach blue inner border to the sides and then the top and bottom of the quilt (26" x 26").

4. Attach the white outer borders to the sides and then the top and bottom of the quilt (34" x 34").

Finishing

1. Sandwich, quilt, and bind your quilt with 2½" wide binding strips pieced to measure 150". Our quilt features a feathered wreath in the center block and partial wreaths in the setting triangles. The blocks were stitched in the ditch. The borders showcase a meandering star design.

2. Sign and date your quilt.

Holiday Blooms Table Mats

Represent your favorite holiday with these delightful table mats. Make a set that can be changed out for each season.

Finished size 16½" x 16½"

Materials
• Scrap for center fabric
• Fat quarter for background fabric
• Fat quarter for outer points
• Scraps for inner points
• Fat quarter for inner border
• Fat quarter for outer border
• Fat quarter for binding

Cutting
From the center fabric (G):
   1: 4½" square

From the background fabric (D):
   1: 3¼" square
   8: 1½" x 2½" rectangles
   4: 2½" squares

From the outer point fabric (F):
   8: 1½" squares
   2: 3¼" squares

From the inner point fabric (E):
   1: 3¼" square
   4: 1½" squares

From the inner border fabric:
   2: 1½" x 8½" strips
   2: 1½" x 10½" strips

From the outer border fabric:
   2: 3½" x 10½" strips
   2: 3½" x 16½" strips

From the binding fabric:
   2: 2½" x width of fabric

Directions

1. Following Steps 1 – 16 on pages 20-21, create a Sunflower block (8½" x 8½").

2. Sew inner borders to the sides and then the top and bottom of the block (10½" x 10½").

3. Sew outer borders to the sides and then the top and bottom of the mat (16½" x 16½").

Finishing

1. Sandwich, quilt, and bind your mats with 2½" wide binding strips pieced to measure 80". Quilt as desired. The center is an ideal place to show off a feathered wreath.

2. Sign and date your quilt.

Reflecting Squares Quilt

A variation on the simple Corner block provides another stunning yet simple project. The striped sashings provide added interest.

Finished size 64½" x 76½"

Materials
- Fat quarter of 11 lights
- Fat quarter of 11 darks
- 1 yard gold
- Black stripe
- Black border
- Fat quarter rust
- 1 yard yellow
- 1¾ yards black stripe
- 2 yards black floral

Cutting
From each of the 11 darks:
  1: 8½" square
  2: 7¼" squares, cut once on the diagonal

From each of the 11 lights:
  4: 4½" squares

From the gold:
  4: 4½" x 12½" rectangles
  6: 2½" x width of fabric (pieced together for inner border)
  16: 3½" squares

From the rust:
  2: 4½" x 12½" rectangles

From the yellow:
  6: 4½" x 12½" rectangles
  8: 2½" x width of fabric (for binding)

From the black stripe:
  2: 6½" x 60½" (cut lengthwise)

From the black floral:
  4: 6½" squares
  2: 6½" x 52½" (cut lengthwise)
  2: 6½" x 64½" (cut lengthwise)

Directions

1. Following Step 3 on page 22, make eleven Corner blocks using a combination of the various lights and darks (8½" x 8½").

2. Center the 7¼" triangles on opposite sides of the Corner blocks. Repeat with the remaining sides. Make 11 (12½" x 12½"). (See page 121 for tips on centering.)

3. Arrange and sew 4½" x 12½" sashing rectangles between four of the blocks. Note color placement. Make 2 (12½" x 60½").

4. Arrange and sew 4½" x 12½" sashing rectangles with the three remaining blocks. Note color placement. Make 1 (12½" x 60½").

5. Alternate block rows with 6½" x 60½" striped sashing (48½" x 60½").

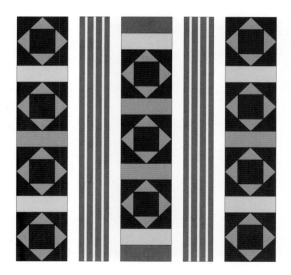

6. Piece the 2½" inner gold borders and cut to size, two 2½" x 52½" and two 2½" x 60½". Attach the inner gold border to the sides and then the top and bottom of the quilt (52½" x 64½").

7. Using the 6½" black floral and 3½" gold squares, follow Step 1 on page 22 to make 4 Corner blocks (6½" x 6½").

8. Attach the black floral borders to the sides of the quilt (64½" x 64½"). Press toward the border. Sew the 6½" Corner blocks to each end of the remaining black floral borders. Press toward the border. Sew the borders to the top and bottom of the quilt (64½" x 76½").

Finishing

1. Sandwich, quilt, and bind your quilt with 2½" wide binding strips pieced to measure 300". The center of each block features a feathered wreath bordered by a fleur de lis. The sashings and inner borders have a wave design, and a wandering feather fills the outer border.

2. Sign and date your quilt.

Cutting Striped Sashings

When cutting striped sashings lengthwise, it is much easier to cut them in one piece than to match the stripes. The extra fabric can be used elsewhere in the blocks, for a scrappy binding, or pieced with other leftovers for the back.

Liberty Square

This little quilt is ideal for a scrappy project. Dig out your leftover half-square triangles or scraps, trim them to size, and have fun!

Finished size 30½" x 30½"

Materials
- ½ yard blue star print
- ¼ yard tan star print
- ¼ yard medium blue print
- ¼ yard dark blue print
- ½ red stripe
- ⅓ yard red star for binding
- Scraps of assorted reds and tans

Cutting
From the blue star print:
  5: 6½" squares
  2: 2½" x 26½" strip
  2: 2½" x 30½" strip
  2: 3" squares

From the tan star print
  20: 3½" squares

From the assorted reds:
  8: 3" squares

From the assorted tans:
  8: 3" squares

From the medium blue:
  4: 3" squares
  4: 2½" x 6½" rectangles

From the dark blue:
  4: 2½" x 18½" strips
  6: 3" squares

From the red stripe:
  4: 2½" x 22½" strips
  4: 3" squares

From the red star:
  4: 2½" x width of fabric
  (for binding)

Directions

1. Following Step 1 on page 22, create five Corner blocks.

2. Using the tan, red, dark blue and medium blue 3" triangles, create 8 medium blue/dark blue, 16 red/tan, 4 red stripe/dark blue, and 4 red stripe/blue star half-square triangles. Trim to 2½".

3. Sew together two red/tan and one medium blue/dark blue half-square triangles as shown. Note orientation. Make four (2½" x 6½").

4. Sew together two red/tan and one medium blue/dark blue half-square triangles as shown. Note orientation. Make four (2½" x 6½").

5. Assemble half-square triangle strips and blue 2½" x 6½" sashing strips as shown. Make 4 (6½" x 6½").

6. Using two Corner squares and one half-square triangle unit, create rows one and three. Make 2 (6½" x 18½").

7. Using one Corner square and two half-square triangle units, create row two. Make 1 (6½" x 18½").

8. Sew the three rows together.

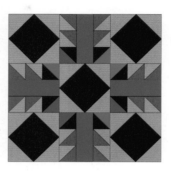

9. Attach the dark blue border to the sides of the quilt. Press toward the dark blue border. Sew a half-square triangle on the end of the remaining border strips. Press toward the border. Sew to the top and bottom. Note the orientation of the corner triangle squares (22½" x 22½").

10. Repeat the same border procedure for the red stripe border. Note the orientation of the triangle square corners (26½" x 26½").

11. Attach the outer blue star border to the top and bottom. Press toward the blue star border. Attach the side borders.

Finishing

1. Sandwich, quilt, and bind your quilt with 2½" wide binding strips pieced to measure 140". Our example has feathered wreaths in the Corner blocks. It was stitched in the ditch around each of the half-square triangles and borders. The medium blue sashing strips have a crosshatch design.

2. Sign and date your quilt.

Grandma's Garden Quilt

Soft and elegant, this simple design provides the perfect opportunity to showcase a large-scale floral or another eye-catching fabric.

Finished size 79½" x 79½"

Materials
• 4 yards white
• 2½ yards floral
• 1¼ yards green
• 1 yard pink
• 1½ yards purple

Cutting
From the white:
  12: 6½" x 22½" rectangles
  24: 6½" x 8½" rectangles
  8: 8½" squares

From the floral:
  4: 8½" x 34½" strips
  8: 8½" squares
  13: 6½" squares
  9: 2½" x width of fabric
  (for binding)

From the green:
  8: 8½" squares
  16: 4½" squares
  28: 3½" squares

From the purple:
  80: 4½" squares

From the pink:
  4: 8½" squares
  16: 4½" squares
  24: 3½" squares

Directions

Note: All corner blocks are made following the directions on page 22.

1. Using the 8½" pink squares and 4½" purple squares, make 4 Corner blocks for the border.

2. Using the 8½" green squares and 4½" purple squares, make 8 Corner blocks for the border.

3. Using the 8½" floral squares and the 4½" pink squares, make 4 Corner blocks.

4. Using the 8½" white squares and 4½" purple squares, make 8 Corner blocks.

5. Using the 8½" floral squares and the 4½" green squares, make 4 Corner blocks.

6. Using the 6½" floral squares and the 3½" green squares, make 7 small Corner blocks.

7. Using the 6½" floral squares and the 3½" pink squares, make 6 small Corner blocks.

8. Arrange the 8½" and 6½" Corner blocks with the white sashing strips as shown. Make two (22½" x 22½").

9. Arrange the 8½" and 6½" Corner blocks with the white sashing strips as shown. Make two (22½" x 22½").

10. Arrange the blocks with the 6½" x 22½" sashing strips as shown. Make 2 (22½" x 50½").

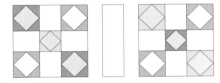

11. Sew a 6½" x 22½" sashing strip to either side of a 6½" floral/green Corner square. Make 1 (6½" x 50½").

12. Sew a 6½" x 22½" sashing strip to either side of a 6½" floral/pink Corner square. Make 4 (6½" x 50½").

13. Sew the sashing strip from Step 11 between the two block rows. Note orientation (50½" x 50½").

14. Sew 2 green/purple 8½" Corner blocks to each end of a floral border strip. Make 4 (8½" x 50½"). Sew this strip to the sashing strip from Step 12 (14½" x 50½").

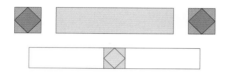

15. Attach one border strip (from step 14) to each side of the center quilt section.

16. Alternate 8½" pink/green and 6½" floral/green Corner squares with 6½" x 8½" sashing strips as shown. Make 4 (14½" x 14½").

17. Sew the double Corner blocks (from Step 16) to each end of the remaining border strips (from Step 14).

18. Sew the top and bottom borders to the quilt.

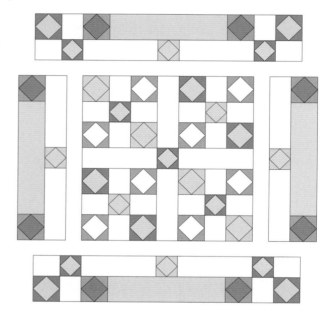

Finishing

1. Sandwich, quilt, and bind your quilt with 2½" wide binding strips pieced to measure 340". Our quilt was machine quilted with an all over rambling rose design.

2. Sign and date your quilt.

General Directions

Quilt	Approximate Size
Baby Quilt	36" x 54"
Lap Throw	54" x 72"
Twin	54" x 90"
Double	72" x 90"
Queen	90" x 108"
King	108" x 108"

Metric Conversion Chart

1/8" = 3 mm	1" = 2.5 cm	7" = 17.8 cm
1/4" = 6 mm	2" = 5.1 cm	8" = 20.3 cm
1/2" = 1.3 cm	3" = 7.6 cm	9" = 22.9 cm
3/4" = 1.9 cm	4" = 10.2 cm	10" = 25.4 cm
7/8" = 2.2 cm	5" = 12.7 cm	11" = 27.9 mm
	6" = 15.2 cm	12" = 30.5 mm

1/8 yd. = 0.11 m	1/2 yd. = 0.46 m
1/4 yd. = 0.23 m	3/4 yd. = 0.69 m
1/3 yd. = 0.3 m	1 yd. = 0.91 m

Approximate Conversion To Metric Formula

When you know:		Multiply by:		To find:
inches (")	x	25	=	millimeters (mm)
inches (")	x	2.5	=	centimeters (cm)
inches (")	x	0.025	=	meters (m)
feet (' or ft.)	x	30	=	centimeters (cm)
feet (' or ft.)	x	0.3	=	meters (m)
yards (yd.)	x	90	=	centimeters (cm)
yards (yd.)	x	0.9	=	meters (m)

Before beginning, read the directions for the chosen pattern in their entirety. Wash all fabric in the manner in which you intend to wash the finished quilt. This preshrinks the fabric and ensures that it is colorfast. Dry fabric and press to remove wrinkles.

Most fabrics are sold as 44" wide from selvedge to selvedge, but many vary slightly in width. Fabric width may also change after the fabric is washed. The materials lists and cutting directions in this book are based on a width of at least 40" of useable fabric after washing and after the selvedges have been trimmed.

Backing fabric and batting dimensions listed are for hand quilting or for quilting on a home sewing machine. Professional quilters using a longarm machine may require a larger backing and batting size. If you intend to have someone else quilt your project, consult them regarding backing and backing size. Cut backing fabric and sew pieces together as necessary to achieve the desired size.

Piecing

Quilt patterns require a scant 1/4" seam allowance. Check your accuracy by cutting three pieces 1 1/2" x 4" and sewing them together along the 4" side. Press the seams to one side, and then lay a ruler over the strips on the right side to check the size. Your piece should measure 3 1/2" across, with the center strip measuring exactly 1". If it doesn't, cut new strips, adjust the seams, and repeat until you have your correct measurement. Even if your machine has a 1/4" foot, check the seam allowance in the same way. You may be able to adjust the needle position to make adjustments.

Mark your perfect seam allowance on the machine bed with a marking pen or a piece of tape. (Blue painters tape or black electrical tape work well and will not leave a residue on your machine.) Always use this guide for sewing accurate quilt seams.

Pressing

Press seams flat after each seam is sewn. Open the pieces, holding the darker side in one hand so that the lighter side including the seam is flat on the pressing board. Place the iron on the right side along the seam line, and hold it in place for a few seconds. This will automatically press the seam toward the darker fabric. Pick up the iron and put it down until you have reached the end of the seam.

Remember to press, not iron, the pieces. Ironing is moving the iron in a back and forth motion, which can easily distort small pieces of fabric. Pressing from the right side helps avoid pressing pleats into the seam and distorting the size. Trim as necessary.

Trimming

Many of the blocks in this book are made larger than necessary so that they can be trimmed to the exact size. This allows for the inaccuracies that often occur, no matter how careful the sewer! Check the size of your pieced blocks as you press. The sizes for the pieces are given in parentheses, for example (2½" x 4½"), as you proceed through the patterns. Check the size after you press, and square up the block if necessary. Trimming to size will help keep the pieces square as you sew to the next piece, eliminating excess frustration! Check the seam allowance frequently.

Centering

Find the center of a piece by folding it in half and pinching a fold mark. The top piece should be pinched with wrong sides together. The bottom piece should be pinched with right sides together, forming a "valley". The top fold will fall into the valley, matching the centers.

Strip Piecing

The invention of the rotary cutter introduced a quick and easy method of cutting strips the width of the fabric (WOF). Strip piecing is used for piecing several of the projects in this book, including the *Happy Day Quilt, Hopscotch Quilt,* and *Checkerboard Pillow.*

1. Cut strips the size indicated in the pattern.

2. Place the strips right sides together and sew along the long side. Press toward the darker fabric. Cut pieces from the strips, the size indicated, to be used in blocks.

3. Rearrange the cut segments and sew them back together, as indicated in the pattern.

Half-Square Triangles

To increase accuracy in making half-square triangles, I like to make them a little large and then trim to the size indicated in the pattern.

1. Cut the appropriate squares in half and pair them, right sides together.

2. Chain stitch the pairs of triangles along the bias edge, feeding them into the sewing machine, one pair after the other, without cutting the thread. Be careful when handling and sewing bias edges!

3. Press the half-square triangles flat and cut them apart.

4. Open each half-square triangle, right side up, and press toward the darker fabric as described in the pressing section.

5. Trim each square using a rotary cutter and a small acrylic ruler. Place the diagonal of a small ruler along the seam line. Adjust the ruler so the fabric extends beyond the upper corner of the ruler. Make a cut along the two sides of the ruler. Reposition the fabric and the ruler, and trim to the size needed. When trimming blocks, always try to measure from the center to avoid cutting too much from one side and not enough from the other.

Flip Corners

Sewing along the diagonal of a small square allows you to create a triangle without cutting the fabric on the diagonal, thus avoiding a bias edge and possible distortion. Single, double, and even quadruple flip corners are used in the projects throughout this book.

1. Mark the diagonal on the wrong side of the square with pencil. Position the square so that the diagonal is at the correct angle. Pin in place, right sides together, and sew on the line.

2. Press. Trim away only the underside of the square, fold the triangle over the sewn line, and press away from the triangle. The base acts as a guide for the edge of triangle. Trim as necessary.

This method can be used on squares or rectangles of any size and on as many corners as indicated.

Fusible Appliqué

This method allows you to complete appliqué very quickly. Follow the directions on the fusible product to prepare and attach appliqué pieces. For most fusible products, it is necessary to flip asymmetrical templates right side down before tracing them on the paper side of the fusible web. Finish the edges of fused appliqué pieces by hand using a blanket stitch or by machine using a blanket, satin, or straight stitch.

Appliqué Bias Strips

This method is ideal for making stems and vines.

1. Cut bias strips the width and length indicated. Fold in half, **wrong sides** together, and sew the seam. Handle carefully to avoid stretching. Guide the strip through your machine, letting the machine do the work.

2. Slip a bias bar or a strip of cardboard inside the bias tube. Center the seam line on one side of the cardboard. Press with the cardboard inside the tube and the seam to the back. Remove the cardboard.

3. Arrange the strip as needed. Pin or thread-baste in place. Stitch the edges with matching thread by hand or by machine. A small straight machine stitch is easy to do and will hardly be visible. Fancy machine stitches work well, also.

Pillow Backs

An envelope back is a quick and easy way to finish a pillow.

1. Cut two fabric pieces for the pillow backs, according to the directions. Fold each piece in half, **wrong sides** together, and stitch ⅜" from the fold to secure the edge of each piece.

2. Lay one folded back on top of the other, overlapping the folded edges to equal the measurements of the pillow top. Lay the quilted pillow top, right side down, on the back pieces.

3. Pin the layers together to hold the pieces while stitching around the entire perimeter of the pillow. Turn right side out and insert a pillow form. Tip: Use the next larger size pillow form to ensure a full pillow.

Quilt Hanger

For ease in displaying quilts and wall hangings, a quilt sleeve can be easily made and attached to the back of the project.

1. Cut a strip of fabric 6" wide and 1" shorter than the width of the quilt. Turn under ¼" at each end. Turn again and stitch.

2. Fold the strip in half lengthwise, **wrong sides** together. Press.

3. Machine baste the hanger to the back of the quilt, matching the raw edges of the quilt and the hanger at the top. The binding will cover these raw edges.

4. Slip stitch the folded edge of the hanger to the back of the quilt.

Note: Flat "screen" molding from the lumber yard makes an ideal hanger. It is inexpensive and can be easily cut to size.

Label

Use a permanent fabric marking pen to sign the quilt back or create a personal label for the quilt. The label can be as simple or elaborate as you choose, but be sure to include your name, address, date, and any other pertinent information that might interest future generations. A simple label can be made with a square of muslin.

1. Cut a 6" muslin square. Fold it in half on the diagonal. Press.

2. Place the triangle in a lower corner of the back of your quilt, **before** attaching the binding. Line up the raw edges of the triangle with the raw edges of the quilt. Pin in place.

3. When you attach the binding, be sure to catch the label edges as well.

4. Slip stitch the folded edge of the hanger to the back of the quilt.

Binding Strips

Quilts with straight edges can be bound with binding strips cut with the grain of the fabric. Cut binding strips the width specified in the quilt pattern, and sew them together with diagonal seams in the following way:

1. Place two binding strips right sides together and perpendicular to each other, aligning the ends as shown. Mark a line on the top strip, from the upper left edge of the bottom strip to the lower right edge of the top strip, and stitch on the marked line.

2. Trim the seam allowance ¼" beyond the stitching, open up the strips, and press the seam allowance open. When all the binding strips have been stitched together, fold the strip in half lengthwise (wrong side in) and press.

Bias Bindings

Plaids and stripes make for interesting bindings when they are cut on the bias. Cut bias strips by aligning the 45° line on a rotary cutting ruler with the bottom edge of the fabric and cutting along the ruler's edge.

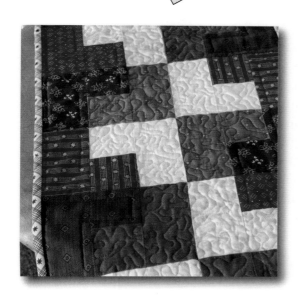

Attaching the Binding

Hint: Using a walking foot to apply binding ensures that all the layers are fed through evenly, reducing distortion or waving.

1. Leaving at least 6" of the binding strip free and beginning several inches away from a corner of the quilt top, align the raw edges of the binding with the edge of the quilt top. Using a standard ¼" seam allowance, stitch the binding to the quilt, stopping and backstitching exactly ¼" from the corner of the quilt top.

2. Remove the quilt from the sewing machine, turn the quilt so the stitched portion of the binding is away from you, and fold the binding away from the quilt, forming a 45° angle on the binding.

Hint: When the angle is correct, the unstitched binding strip will be aligned with the next edge of the quilt top.

3. Maintaining the angled corner fold, fold the loose binding strip back down, aligning this fold with the stitched edge of the quilt top and the raw edge of the binding with the adjacent quilt top edge. Stitch the binding to the quilt beginning at the fold, backstitching to secure the seam.

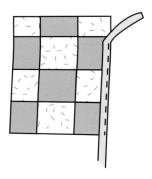

4. Continue attaching the binding in the same manner until you are 6" from the first stitching. Then, fold both loose ends of the binding strip back upon themselves so that the folds meet in the center of the unstitched section of the binding, and crease the folds.

5. Measure the width of the folded binding strip. Cut both ends of the binding strip that measurement beyond the creased folds. (For example: If the quilt pattern instructed you to cut the binding strips 2½" wide, the folded binding strip would measure 1¼". In this case, you would cut both ends of the binding strip 1¼" beyond the creased folds.)

6. Open up both ends of the binding strip and place them right sides together and perpendicular to each other as shown. Mark a line on the top strip from the upper left corner of the top strip to the lower right corner of the bottom strip. Pin the strips together and stitch on the marked line.

7. Refold the binding strip and place it against the quilt top to test the length. Open the binding strip back up, trim the seam allowance ¼" beyond the stitching, and finger press the seam allowance open. Refold the binding strip, align the raw edges with the edge of the quilt top, and finish stitching it to the quilt.

8. Trim the batting and backing ⅜" beyond the binding stitching. Fold the binding to the back of the quilt, and blind stitch it to the backing fabric, covering the machine stitching. Keep your stitches small and close together. When you reach a corner, stitch the mitered binding closed on the back side of the quilt, and pass the needle through the quilt to the right side. Stitch the mitered binding closed on the front side of the quilt, and pass the needle back through the quilt to the back side. Continue stitching the folded edge of the binding to the back of the quilt.

Acknowledgments

We all know that group effort makes a large project come together more quickly. This project came together without meetings but with the support of friends who offered their time and skills to make the deadline a reality.

Nicole Gould, friend and editor, was instrumental in keeping me on schedule and making the final result a book we can all be proud to share with others.

Quilters Bonnie Erickson, Julie Schrader, Karla Schulz, Marilyn Nikolaus, and Pat Bley; and finishers Joann Fenelon, Carol Johnson, Mary Jo Kurten, Sheila Lee, Ida Philips, Terry Ralston, and Sheila Stanley all worked with expertise and quickness, for which I am truly grateful.

Mike and Rhonda Hicks of the Mountain Thyme Bed & Breakfast Inn, Jessieville, Arkansas, provided generous hospitality and a lovely setting for photographing the quilts. (Visit their website at www.mountainthyme.com.)

David Corbell and Deborah Warren of Double D Photoworks, Hot Springs, Arkansas, worked quickly and tirelessly to produce the beautiful photographs shown throughout this book. (Visit their website at www.doubledphotoworks.com.)

Thanks to all the Plum Creek Quilters, especially Lynn Roberts and her quilting buddy Pam Minsch, for their continued enthusiasm for the art of quiltmaking.

Thanks also to Bev Keltgen and Carol Newman, who have brought support and humor to Plum Creek Patchwork for many years.

Special thanks to my husband, Ormon, who didn't know what he was getting into years ago on the prairie when he set up my first quilt frame as a winter blizzard was approaching. Without his support and that of the quilters I have met along the way, none of this would have been possible.

Johanna and Ormon Wilson

About the Author

Johanna Wilson began quilting in 1984 during a winter storm on the Minnesota prairie. Housebound, she picked up an old quilt top that a friend had passed on to her, and the rest is quilting history.

Through the years, Johanna has created projects for numerous patterns and books, designed fabrics, and taught all over the country. Teaching is one of her great loves, and she delights in hearing that her students are passing on their love of quilting to others.

For six years, Johanna hosted an annual quilt retreat in Minnesota that drew quilters from all over the United States and Canada. Beginning and expert quilters alike completed a sampler quilt and shared their love of quilting. The group continues to meet each summer, now hosted by one of Johanna's former students.

A frequent contributor to *The Quilter* and *Fabric Trends* magazines, *Garden Medley Quilts* is Johanna's first book published by All American Crafts.